WILDLY WEIRD
BUT TOTALLY TRUE

ANIMALS OF THE WORLD

Fun Facts, True Stories and Trivia

Copyright © 2023 Seana Smith

All rights reserved.

No portion of this book may be reproduced in any form without written permission from the publisher or author, except as permitted by U.S. copyright law.

This publication is designed to provide accurate and authoritative information in regard to the subject matter covered. It is sold with the understanding that neither the author nor the publisher is engaged in rendering legal, investment, accounting or other professional services. While the publisher and author have used their best efforts in preparing this book, they make no representations or warranties with respect to the accuracy or completeness of the contents of this book and specifically disclaim any implied warranties of merchantability or fitness for a particular purpose. No warranty may be created or extended by sales representatives or written sales materials. The advice and strategies contained herein may not be suitable for your situation. You should consult with a professional when appropriate. Neither the publisher nor the author shall be liable for any loss of profit or any other commercial damages, including but not limited to special, incidental, consequential, personal, or other damages.

Illustrations + Book Cover by Joy Lora and Seana Smith

1st edition 2023

ISBN 9798860346116

Contents

1. Astounding African animals — 1
2. Funky farm animals — 15
3. Daft dogs and crazy cats — 34
4. Brilliant birds — 43
5. Spectacular spiders, insects and scorpions — 51
6. Unlikely lizards — 62
7. Strange sea creatures — 71
8. More marvellous mammals — 81

About the author — 93

Also in the series — 94

Astounding African Animals

Did you know that no two elephant ears are the same? Just as no two humans have unique fingerprints, no elephants have exactly the same ears.

Elephants have huge ears so that they can hear sounds from up to six miles away and they can hear sounds that we humans cannot. Elephants can hear extremely low noises, such as a rumbling in the earth, as well as extremely high sounds, such as a bird tweeting. They can even hear sounds that we can't hear because they are too high or too low.

Elephants utilise their ears for other purposes as well, such as cooling down on hot days. Elephants, unlike humans, cannot sweat, therefore they must find other methods to remain cool. Their large ears contain many blood vesselss, and, as they flap their ears, their blood cools and helps to cool their entire body.

Elephants use their super-hearing to communicate with one another. They generate low-pitched sounds that humans cannot hear, but other elephants can hear these sounds from long distances.

Elephants ears are also used to demonstrate an elephant's size and strength. When they are attempting to appear tough, they extend their ears wide.

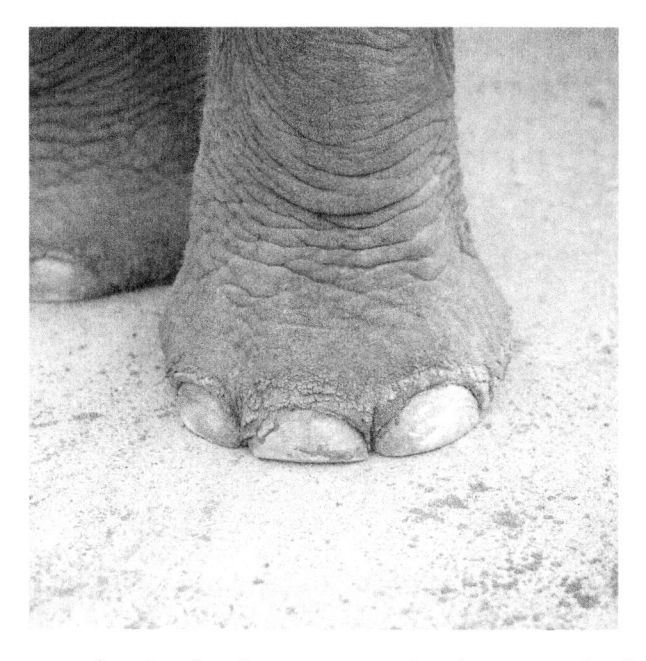

And, guess what? Elephants can also hear with their feet. Elephants can detect vibrations made by other animals from up to 20 kilometres away.

Elephants are the largest land animals on the planet, so it's only logical that elephants have enormous feet to support their vast weight. The average elephant foot is around 19 inches long and broad, with a circumference of more than 4 feet.

Each elephant's foot contains five toes, although not all of them have nails. Both the African elephant and the Asian elephant have five toes on their front feet and four on their rear feet. Elephants walk using their toes for balance and to assist them grasp the ground, just as humans do.

Elephant feet are flat because each heel has a big pad of gristle that functions as a shock absorber and allows elephants to walk gently.

Their legs are significantly straighter than those of other animals and can easily sustain their weight. Elephants spend the majority of their lives travelling large distances, and their feet have evolved to accommodate this lifestyle.

Elephants maintained in zoos or limited areas, on the other hand, may acquire foot illnesses or arthritis owing to a lack of frequent mobility.

Trunk facts

- Elephants can suck up to 2.2 gallons of water in their trunks, then squirt it over their backs to keep cool.

- They use their trunks to defend themselves and push obstacles out of their path. Large elephants can lift items weighing over 650 lbs with their trunks.

- The trunk is a combination of the elephant's

nose and upper lip and is used for smelling and also for breathing, especially when they are walking through water.

- Elephants use their trunks to rip tree bark, burrow into the ground for water, and snap huge limbs off trees.

- The trunk is also sensitive and elephants use their trunks to wipe and clean their eyes.

- The elephant trunk is made up of about 40,000 distinct muscles rather than bones, giving it an extraordinary range of motion.

Giraffes are mammals and so you might expect them to be able to swim well. In fact, giraffes actively avoid water and they never swim, because they cannot. Due to their long necks, long and heavy legs, and their relatively small body, giraffes are simply not adapted to float or swim.

Giraffes do not even drink water very often. They are herbivores and the grass, fruit, roots and leaves they eat hold moisture. When they do drink, they need to splay their front legs wide and then bend their long necks down. Not very elegant!

The giraffe's horns are another unusual feature. Baby giraffes are born with horn-like structures which are actually bone protrusions called ossicones.

The ossicones are not actual horns because they lack a keratin sheath. These ossicones are really hardened cartilage coated with skin. Male and female giraffes both have ossicones.

During fights and defence, male giraffes use their ossicones as weapons, while their heads serve as clubs. The ossicones increase weight and focus the power of impact onto a limited area, allowing the giraffe to deliver stronger blows with higher contact pressure.

Baby giraffes tumble down from their mothers who stand when giving birth. The mother then licks her baby, and within about an hour the giraffe calf can stand up and stretch its 6 ft body up to start to suckle its mother's milk.

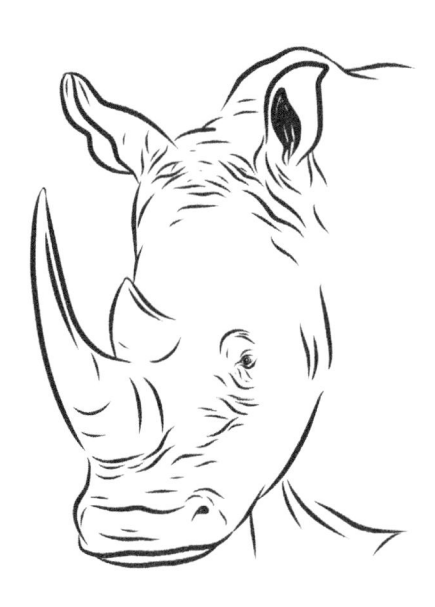

Did you know that the horn of the rhinoceros is unique? It is not made of bone at all but of keratin, the same material that makes up humans' hair and nails.

Most animal horns have a bone core covered by a thin covering of keratin, but rhino horns are remarkable in that they are made of keratin alone. This makes them more comparable in composition to human hair and nails than to other animal horns.

Rhinoceros horns are not embedded in the skull. Since the horns of rhinos are made entirely of keratin and not bone, they are biodegradable.

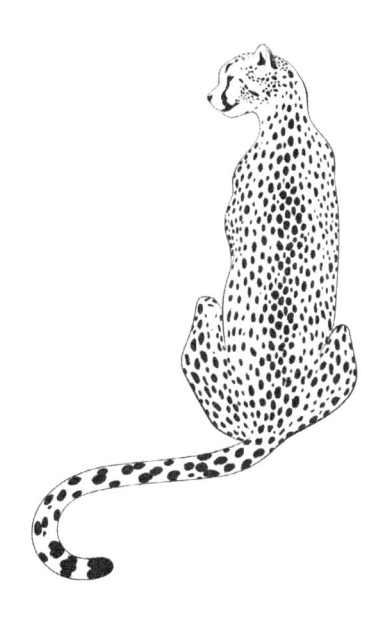

Cheetahs use their tail to sprint at breakneck speeds!

Cheetahs have long, muscular tails that act like a rudder on a boat, assisting them in steering and balancing their bodyweight when running.

Cheetahs must be able to perform rapid, abrupt twists and turns without losing their balance when running after their prey. This is when the tail comes into play. Cheetahs can alter their body motions and maintain their balance while running just by swinging their tails back and forth.

However, the tail does more than merely aid in balance. During high-speed chases, the flattened tip of the tail works as a rudder, steering the cheetah in the right direction. A cheetah uses its tail to control its body and keep it on track, similar to how a captain uses a rudder to navigate a ship.

The cheetah's tail can grow to be 33 inches long, which is around two-thirds of its total length. That's quite a tail. Cheetahs have little contact with the ground during sprints, therefore they rely on their tails to keep them balanced and steady as they run.

Cheetahs whip their tails from side to side to keep their bodies' centre of gravity aligned, similar to humans moving their arms when running.

Did you know that the eye of an ostrich is larger than its brain and the biggest of any existing land mammal, measuring five centimetres wide?

The common ostrich from Africa has the largest eyes of any animal that lives on land. Its eyes are around the size of a billiard ball and five times the size of a human eye. Close inspection reveals that ostrich eyes are extremely lovely, with lengthy eyelashes to shield them.

Ostriches rely on their huge eyes to protect them from predators they may meet on the African savannah. Even though they have wings, they cannot fly like other birds, but they compensate by being extremely quick runners. They can reach speeds of up to 45 mph. This allows them to outrun many predators.

The ostrich's enormous eyeballs aid them in this endeavour. During the day, they can see things up to 1.8 miles away. They can see anything up to 165 ft distant at night. That's approximately the length of a basketball court.

The ostrich, which is the world's biggest bird, also has the largest feet in relation to its overall size of all the creatures in the animal kingdom. The ostrich is the only bird with two toes. The ostrich's inner toe resembles a hoof rather than a toe, and it has a huge claw on it.

Ostriches use their wings as rudders when sprinting to assist them change direction. And be careful! Those legs can potentially be used as lethal weapons. A human or a predator, such as a lion, can be killed by an ostrich kick.

Funky farm animals

Did you know that chickens are the closest living relatives to dinosaurs? Whilst scientists were unable to extract DNA from ancient dinosaur remains, they did discover molecules of collagen, a structural protein, within a T-rex bone.

When scientists compared it to modern creatures, they found that chickens and ostriches were the closest matches, with alligators coming in second.

The colour of a chicken's earlobe determines the colour of her eggs. If a hen has red earlobes, she'll lay brown eggs, while hens with white earlobes lay white eggs.

Whatever the colour of the egg, the nutritional content and taste are the same, whatever the shell colour. If you find that brown eggs are more expensive, it is likely to be because the breed of hen that lays them is larger and so eats more feed than the breeds which lay white eggs.

A chicken has a peak speed of 9 miles per hour and can run a mile in around six minutes and forty seconds. Even though they can run at top speeds, they do not sweat. To cool off, they will sip water or flap their wings to disperse body heat, and sometimes even pant.

When chicks are ready to hatch, they use their egg tooth to help them break free from their shell. This egg tooth is a small, bumpy protrusion on the top of their beak. A few days after hatching, the chick no longer needs the egg tooth and it naturally falls off.

If you have ever thought that a duck looks half asleep, you might be right. Generally, ducks sleep with one eye open and one closed. In fact, only half of their brain sleeps at a time, whilst the other half of the brain is awake, and so the eye is open. This is an excellent way to rest whilst staying alert for predators.

Ducks often live in groups, and the ducks on the outside of the group tend to sleep with half of the brain, whilst those in the centre can close both eyes and enjoy a whole brain sleep.

Did you know that ducks are pretty fast flyers? On average, they can reach speeds of about 50 mph, which is even faster than the legendary sprinter Usain Bolt who ran as fast as 27.33 mph.

However, not all ducks are skilled fliers. Welsh Harlequin ducks for instance are flightless and can only get about 12 inches off the ground at most. They can only move forward a couple of feet during their flight attempts.

Some ducks can achieve even greater speeds. A red-breasted merganser was once recorded flying at a whopping 100 mph. That's about 40 mph faster than a cheetah, the fastest land animal in the world!

Ducks' feet don't freeze in icy waters thanks to a clever system called countercurrent blood exchange. Warm blood flows from the heart to their feet, while cold blood from the feet returns to the heart.

The arteries and veins carrying this blood are close together, helping regulate temperature. The blood in the duck's feet is cool by the time it gets to the feet so there is not a reduced blood flow and so no frostbite.

Ducks have a special gland near their tails called the preen gland. This gland produces a special oil. When ducks preen, they gather this oil and spread it all over their feathers, as if they are applying a waterproof coating. This oil coating keeps the water from seeping in, so they can swim happily without getting soggy.

A duck's bill is incredibly sensitive, just like our fingertips and palms. The bones in the duck's beak are connected to their skull, and the tip of the beak is packed with blood vessels and nerve endings. This makes the tip of their beak very sensitive to pain, and if it gets injured it can bleed easily.

While all ducks can dive, some species are better at it than others. The long-tailed duck, also known as the oldsquaw, is a champion diver among waterbirds. It can dive as deep as 240 feet.

Cows' nose prints are as unique as fingerprints!

Just like human fingerprints and the skins of an elephant's ear, each cow's nose is as unique as a human fingerprint. In fact, cows' nose prints have been used to identify individual cows. A scientist called Petersen wrote an article in 1922 that was the first to formally acknowledge that each cow has a unique nose print and that these could be used for identification.

Of course, cattle used to be branded, and tattoos were also used. Sometimes ears were given notches, drawings were made of cattle colouring, or photos were taken. Nowadays most cattle have ear tags. However, the fact remains that their nose prints are unique and can be used as and when necessary.

Computer systems have been developed so that farmers can take photos of their cows' noses and then put the photos into a computer system to create a unique identification from the markings on the noses.

We don't tend to think of cows as being lively or wide-awake creatures, however, unlike humans, cows don't require much sleep. On average, they only spend about 30 minutes in deep sleep per day, which is divided into 6 to 10 short periods. However, they do spend a significant amount of time lying down, up to 10 hours each day.

Sheep have rectangular pupils in their eyes! These rectangular pupils provide them with an incredible field of vision, spanning approximately 270 to 320 degrees. This means that sheep can see almost everything around them, except for directly behind them, without needing to turn their heads.

This exceptional peripheral vision is vital for their survival as prey animals, allowing them to stay vigilant and spot potential predators, even while grazing with their heads down.

Other animals with rectangular pupils include goats, cows, octopuses, deer, horses, and toads.

Did you know that sheep have a unique feature among grazing animals that is called a philtrum? The philtrum is a groove that divides the upper lip of the sheep into distinct left and right sides.

This adaptation serves a purpose for these selective grazers. Sheep have a preference for vegetation close to the ground, such as leaves and blades rather than stems.

The philtrum allows them to get very close to the soil surface, giving them an advantage over other ruminant animals that cannot graze as low.

Horses can't use their mouth to breathe! Horses are what we call obligate nasal breathers. Unlike humans, they cannot breathe through their mouths, so horses rely solely on their noses for breathing.

Horses have the amazing ability to flare their nostrils, allowing them to take in larger amounts of oxygen. It's their way of compensating for the absence of mouth-breathing.

And, another fascinating horse fact is that horses can sleep standing up. In fact, horses can sleep both standing up and lying down. When they lie down, horses need at least 30 minutes of good sleep to feel fully rested and avoid being sleep-deprived.

Horses have a special "stay-apparatus" that helps them stand without falling over, using tendons and ligaments to lock their legs in position. This lets them rest and save energy while standing, ready to run if they need to.

When horses gallop, the motion could potentially trigger vomiting, making them vulnerable to predators. So, over time, evolution has removed the ability to vomit entirely as a safety adaptation.

Horses also cannot burp. They are very polite creatures. Horses can't burp or vomit like other animals due to their unique digestive system.

The cardiac sphincter is a valve between the stomach and oesophagus which only allows a one-way flow of food.

As a result, when a horse's stomach becomes too full, it cannot release gas through burping or vomiting. This can sometimes lead to digestive issues such as colic which can prove fatal.

Goats sneeze to warn others! Did you know that goats use sneezes as an alarm system? When they sneeze, it's their way of warning other goats about possible danger.

This is a clever strategy because it doesn't alert predators. Since goats stick together in herds, this sneezing behaviour helps keep everyone safe. Of course, goats may also sneeze due to irritation, allergies, or illness.

Have you ever heard of the Tennessee fainting goat? These goats have a unique genetic trait that causes their muscles to freeze up when they get excited or startled.

This often causes the goat to topple over. It may look like they're fainting, but the goats are actually fully conscious during these episodes. After a short time, their muscles relax and they're back on their feet.

This condition, called myotonia congenita, is caused by an inherited disorder affecting the chloride channel in their skeletal muscles. Other names that these goats have been known as include nervous, stiff-legged, myotonic and wooden-leg goats. Poor goats!

Pigs can breathe through their bottoms! Surprising research from Japan suggests that bottoms might play a role in helping animals breathe.

Scientists discovered that pigs can actually absorb oxygen through their anuses, leading to potential treatments for respiratory issues in humans.

Researchers observed that pigs were able to survive without relying on their lungs for breathing after they had introduced oxygen and oxygenated liquid through the pigs' rectums. Even in severe respiratory failure conditions, a 50-kilogram pig could endure for up to 30 minutes using this innovative method. So far this is early research, but there is the potential that this method could also be used for short periods in humans whose lungs are not working.

Pigs are pretty smart animals and scientists have shown that pigs can learn how to play simple video games using a joystick.

In the study, four pigs were taught to use their snouts to control a joystick and move a cursor on a screen. They had to reach target walls for rewards.

This is remarkable because pigs don't have opposable thumbs and they're far-sighted animals. But they managed to do it.

Other studies have also revealed that pigs can learn obedience commands, use mirrors to find hidden food, and even use tools. These findings show that pigs are capable of learning and adapting to different tasks.

Turkey droppings can be used to determine the gender of the bird! So if you are looking at a turkey and wondering whether it is male or female, just stand behind it and wait.

Male turkeys have J-shaped droppings, while female turkeys have spiral-shaped droppings. The size of the droppings can also be used to determine the age of the bird. Older turkeys have larger droppings.

The reason for the difference in dropping shape is due to the different anatomy of male and female turkeys. Male turkeys have a rudimentary phallus in their cloaca, which is the opening through which they excrete waste and reproduce.

This phallus causes the droppings to be J-shaped. Female turkeys do not have a phallus, so their droppings are spiral-shaped.

Another gender giveaway is that male turkeys, or toms, gobble to attract mates during the spring and fall mating seasons.

The gobble is a loud, descending sound that can be heard from far away. Toms also gobble when they are surprised by loud noises or when they are settling in for the night.

Female turkeys, or hens, do not gobble, but they make a variety of other sounds, including purrs, yelps and kee-kees.

Turkeys can make at least 30 different calls, which they use to communicate with each other about food, danger, and other important information.

The biggest gender giveaway though is the turkey's tail. Male turkeys have exuberant tail feathers which they like to fan up. Females are much more modest and do not extend their tail feathers.

Daft dogs and crazy cats

Did you know your dog's paws may smell like Fritos, popcorn, or Doritos because of a bacteria? Yes, some dogs have "Frito Feet" or paws that smell like our favourite snacks. So, what causes this? It turns out that the culprits are bacteria called pseudomonas and proteus. When mixed with perspiration and moisture on your dog's paws, these bacteria can produce a cheesy or corn-chip-like odour.

But don't worry, a slight cheese or snack-like odour on their paws is entirely typical for dogs. They pick up a lot of microbes since their paws are continuously in contact with the ground.

When they sweat, germs and moisture combine to produce that delectable fragrance. However, if your dog's paws begin to stink, or if you observe redness, pus, inflammation, dryness, or scaling, you should have them checked out by a veterinarian.

While dogs sweat through the merocrine sweat glands in their paws, excessive sweating might indicate an underlying problem. Because dogs lack a large number of sweat glands, they must rely on other methods to regulate their body temperature, such as panting and artery dilatation.

So, the next time you smell Fritos or popcorn emanating from your pup's paws, you'll know it's simply their natural aroma and nothing to be concerned about.

We all know that dogs wag their tails, but it turns out that watching their ears is also an important way of getting to know how your dog is feeling. Dog communicate how they feel to other dogs and to humans by using their ears, faces, bodies, tails, and even their smell.

For example, if a dog's ears are flattened against its head, that might indicate that it is fearful or uncertain. However, if its ears are pointed up, that might indicate that the dog is attentive, enthusiastic and ready to play.

It is critical to pay attention to dogs' body language. Dogs can hear things that humans cannot. They will sometimes react to sounds that we cannot hear. You may see your dog's ears pointing forward and notice it snarling or barking. This might indicate that your dog has heard something that makes it feel intimidated or terrified.

Even though dogs have stronger hearing than humans, they have difficulty hearing low-pitched sounds. Because women's voices are normally higher, a dog may have an easier time hearing a woman's voice than a man's.

Cats are famous for their eyes, and especially for the vertical pupils they have. Many animals associated as prey have horizontal pupils while many small predators, like cats, have vertical pupils.

A group of experts discovered that animals with vertical pupils that resemble slits are generally predators who prefer to conceal and spring out to attack their prey from a short distance. These predators must be able to see how far away their prey is in order to pounce at the appropriate time.

The vertical pupils aid them in surprise pounce-attacks. Ambush and nocturnal predators must properly calculate the distance to their prey, and the vertical slits possess optical properties that make them ideal for that. However, this rule only applies if the animal is short and its eyes are not too high off the ground.

While cats and foxes have vertical slits, bigger predators such as lions, wolves, and tigers have round pupils. We humans also have round pupils. Similar to bigger predators, this is because of our height.

Did you know your cat's tail is an extension of its spine, and cats use them to communicate their mood? One of the most fascinating aspects of a cat's tail is that it aids in balance.

While you observe your kitty travelling through small fences or high spots, its tail is working hard to function as a counterweight, allowing it to stay balanced and accurate while pouncing on prey.

A straight-up tail indicates greeting, a bend at the tip indicates relaxation, and a puffed up tall tail indicates dominance or confrontation. And if you notice your cat flicking its tail quickly, it might signify it's about to pounce.

Remember that a cat's tail is a very delicate and necessary feature of its body. If your cat's tail is hurt, it can lead to serious health concerns such as movement difficulty, incontinence, or nerve damage.

Lions cannot purr, did you know that? We all know that domestic cats purr, and, in fact, some larger members of the cat family can purr too, like cheetahs, pumas, bobcats and lynxes.

Lions, tigers, leopards and jaguars cannot purr, but they do roar very loudly. The big cats that purr cannot roar at all.

All of the cats, large and small, have a bone in the throat called the hyoid which supports the larynx and the tongue. In the purring cats, this bone is rigid whereas in the cats that roar this bone is more flexible and has a more elastic ligament. This is what produces the roar.

Purring is produced from a cat's larynx, cats constrict the section of the larynx which touches the vocal cords producing vibrations which we humans hear as purring.

Remarkably the purring sound can be heard both when cats breath in and when they breath out. But why do cats purr? Is it only because they are happy?

No, the most recent scientific research has shown that cats purr when they are happy, and also when they are hungry, and most owners can tell the difference between these types of purring.

Cats might also purr when they are hurt or unwell. There is early research suggesting that the vibrations of the purring help heal wounds.

Who would have guessed that cats could be so complicated?

Brilliant Birds

OWLS ARE FAMOUS FOR their enormous eyes and their remarkable night vision, but did you know that owls also have amazing hearing capacity?

Remarkably, some owls have crooked ears meaning that the ear opening on one side of the head is higher than on the other.

This may appear unusual but it aids them in determining the height and direction of a sound. When a sound reaches the owl's asymmetrical ears, the brain receives two slightly distinct impulses allowing it to locate the sound's position.

Because its left ear entrance is higher than its right, if a barn owl hears a sound originating from below its line of sight it will be louder in its right ear.

The owl's brain then instantaneously integrates the impulses to form a mental representation of where the sound source is situated.

Barn owls have the finest hearing of any animal ever studied. They may not see as well as other animals in dim light but their ears more than compensate.

Did you know that owls have night vision capabilities? In fact, they see better in the dark! Owls have large eyes that are densely packed with light-sensitive cells, allowing them to see at night with only minimal light.

Owls' eyes have some differences from human eyes that allow them to see better in the dark. They have a particular layer of cells called the tapetum lucidum, which reflects light back into their eyes and allows them to see better in the dark.

Owls also have more rods in their eyes, which are cells that aid in low-light vision. Their eyeballs can also move far more freely than ours, allowing them to view in different directions without turning their heads.

Contrary to popular belief, owls cannot see in complete darkness. They can, however, see in as little as one-hundredth the amount of light that humans require to see clearly.

As a result, their vision is 10 to 100 times greater than ours. All of these characteristics combine to make owls excellent niocturnal hunters. They can detect even the slightest movements in the dark, allowing them to locate and capture their prey.

The mighty eagle also has amazing eyesight. Eagles have huge eyes and can spot prey as tiny as a rabbit from 1.8 miles away. That's like spotting a little insect crawling on the ground from the top of a ten-story building.

Eagles' eyes include a large number of unique cells that allow them to see extremely effectively. They have up to a million light-sensitive cells per square millimetre of retina, five times more than humans.

Furthermore, they contain two specific cells called foveae that assist them in sharpening their images.

Eagles have three eyelids to keep their eyes clean. The two eyelids on the outside of the eye are the ones we normally see.

Because the bottom eyelid of eagles is larger than the top eyelid, they blink up rather than down.

The name given to the third eyelid, an inner eyelid, is the nictitating membrane.

This membrane is clear and operates from the side like a windscreen wiper.

Birds' wing facts

- Owls have feathers that are specially adapted to allow for silent flight, allowing them to swoop down on their prey without being heard.

- Flamingos are born with grey feathers but their feathers turn pink due to the carotenoid pigments found in their diet of shrimp, algae and crustaceans.

- The wings of the pigeon are adapted for sustained flight, with the bird being able to fly for long distances at a steady pace without tiring.

- The wings of the seagull are adapted for gliding, so that this bird can soar for long periods of time without flapping its wings.

- The wings of the penguin are modified into flippers, which enable the bird to swim and dive through water.

- The albatross has the longest wingspan of any bird, up to 11 feet from wingtip to wingtip. The wings of the albatross are so powerful that the bird can stay in the air for months at a time without visiting land. A tracked albatross once flew right around the world in only 46 days.

Spectacular spiders, insects and scorpions

S PIDERS ARE FAMOUS FOR being busy creatures, but who knew spiders do not sleep? Spiders do not close their eyes like humans do since they do not have eyelids.

Instead, spiders relax and preserve energy by lowering their activity levels and metabolic rates. This is especially beneficial for the spiders that weave webs to catch their prey, as they may have to wait a long time between meals.

Spiders have eight eyes on average (some have six or less), with two large ones in front that let them see well and assess distance, and two smaller ones on the sides that sense movement. Though spiders have many eyes, only a few have strong vision.

To navigate and discover their prey, they rely on touch, vibration and taste inputs. Many spiders are more active at night to avoid being eaten by other creatures that are more active during the day, such as birds.

Jumping spiders are a type of spider with eight eyes, and are especially fascinating since they have incredible vision and can even see behind themselves. Their eyes act as a team, with each pair performing a separate function.

They monitor their prey with all of their eyes and calculate the distance before jumping to seize it. Did you know jumping spiders can jump more than 20 times their own body length? That's equivalent to a human leaping over a whole basketball court.

Bees have amazing eyesight and that is partly because they have five eyes, two large ones on the side of the head, and three little eyes on top.

The large eyes are compound eyes and they are responsible for the majority of the bee's vision. Each compound eye has thousands of microscopic lenses known as facets, which capture little portions of what the bee is looking at.

The bee's brain then combines all of these signals to form a complete picture. These qualities allow bees to see colour and objects from a very broad angle.

Bees have a different perspective on the world than humans. Bees can see blue, green and ultraviolet light, whereas humans can only perceive red, blue and green. So bees cannot see red, but they can see ultraviolet light.

This is really important for them since they can discern patterns on flower petals and this helps bees in their search for nectar-rich blooms.

Bees, despite their keen vision, cannot see very far. They are nearsighted, which means their focus is fixed and cannot be adjusted based on the distance of the thing they are looking at.

However, bees compensate for this by being able to perceive things while in motion. They can detect motions that occur at 1/300th of a second and view the environment five times quicker than humans.

Dragonflies literally do have eyes in the back of their head. They feature two large complex eyes with thousands of lenses each, as well as three simple or basic eyes called ocelli.

Dragonfly eyes are so large they almost cover the whole head, meaning the dragonfly can see all around them, except for a small area right at their rear.

Their eyes are separated on either side of their skull and join at the top. They view the world as a mosaic of a million little images.

Dragonflies can detect colours that humans cannot, as well as various tints and intensities of those hues, including ultraviolet light.

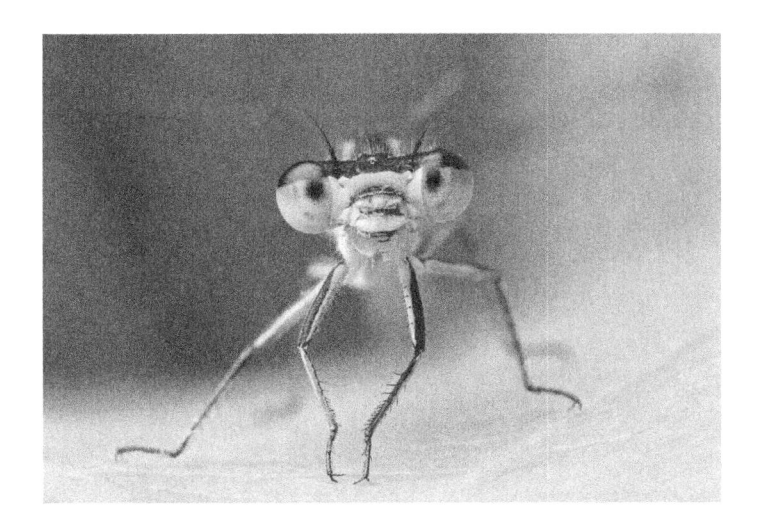

Dragonfly eyes are made up of over 100 million microscopic lenses known as ommatidia. Each of these has a reflective mirror-type surface that reflects light back into the eye, where it is focused by the retina, which then integrates the images from all ommatidia into a single image that is processed in the brain.

Dragonflies can perceive objects as close to their eyes as one-hundredth of an inch! Even at close range, this is significantly greater than humans can see.

They can also sense the presence of food and predators in the water by seeing ultraviolet light. Dragonflies have excellent night vision and can see well in low light or full darkness. Dragonflies utilise their sight to travel and identify prey.

Dragonflies have an exceptionally acute sense of sight, with a retina capable of concentrating on things 40 times closer than humans can detect.

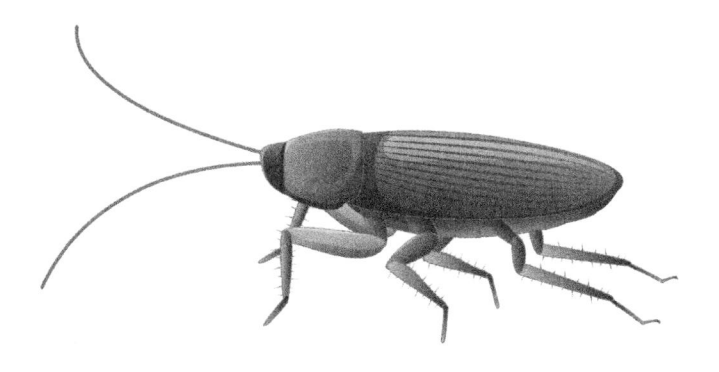

Did you know that cockroaches don't have ears? Many people believe that cockroaches have ears in their knees. It's not true, but it's easy to understand how people may confuse them with crickets, which do have ears on their knees.

Even though cockroaches lack hearing they can detect vibrations in the air and on the ground. Cockroaches have two small organs on their abdomens which are called cerci. These are able to sense even very slight movements in the air, alerting them to predators.

They also use their antennae to smell and feel their way around, and their legs are coated in ultra-sensitive hairs that let them detect even the smallest contact. Because cockroaches can detect vibrations, they dislike loud noises such as clapping, slamming doors, or stomping.

They may examine the source of the noise to check if there is food nearby, but they are more likely to hide until the vibrations stop.

Some people have tried using sound to repel cockroaches, but it doesn't seem to work very well. Despite the fact that cockroaches can detect vibrations, research has proven that ultrasonic devices neither kill nor repel them.

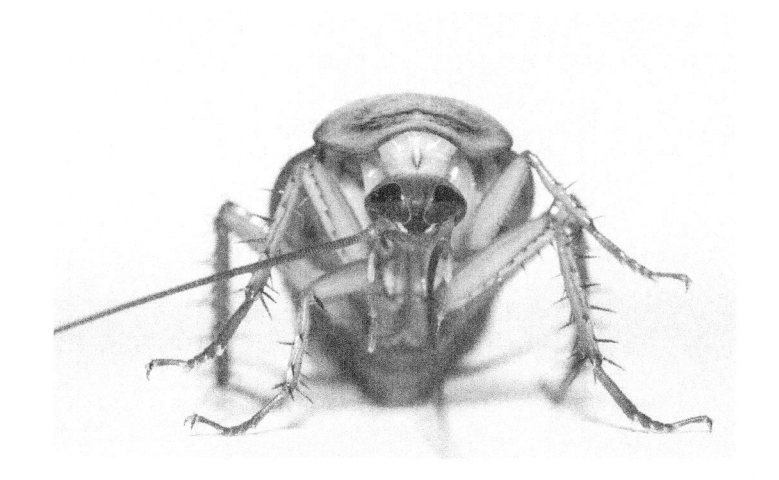

Cockroaches have amazing eyes that are placed on top of their heads and have a nearly 360-degree view of their surroundings. Each of their eyes have more than 1,000 lenses, so they can see many things at the same time.

Scorpions can pick one of the several poisons in their tail depending on what they're up against. Other animals have a single kind of venom but scorpions can choose between neurotoxins and cardiotoxins, as well as nephrotoxins and hemolytic toxins, plus a variety of other chemicals such as histamine, serotonin and tryptophan.

Some poisons are more effective on specific sorts of animals than others, therefore scorpions have to be smart about when and how they deploy their venom.

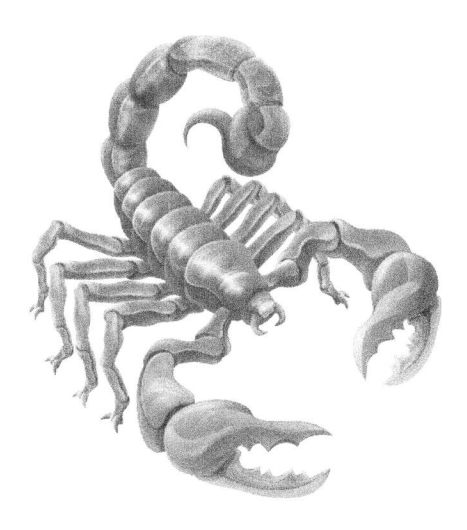

Scorpions are formidable not just because of their poisons. They are also survival experts. When food is scarce, a scorpion can reduce its metabolism to the point that it only needs to consume one bug a year.

They can also survive in extremely harsh settings, whether hot or cold. Researchers have even frozen scorpions overnight and seen them defrost and walk away as if nothing had happened.

Unlikely lizards

Geckos lick their eyes to clean them – yuk! Geckos have adapted to the lack of eyelids by cleaning and moistening their eyes with their mouth and tongue.

This practice allows them to keep their vision clear and avoid eye infections. Not many animals' tongues can reach their eyes and not many can lick their own eyes. Well done, geckos.

With their large eyes, geckos have a broad range of vision, which is important for identifying predators and prey. Geckos have unique cells in their eyes called rods that are sensitive to low light levels, which allows them to see at night.

Another adaptation that geckos have developed is to go to sleep by narrowing their pupils rather than shutting their eyes. In dry locations, where water is limited, this helps them conserve moisture and keep hydrated.

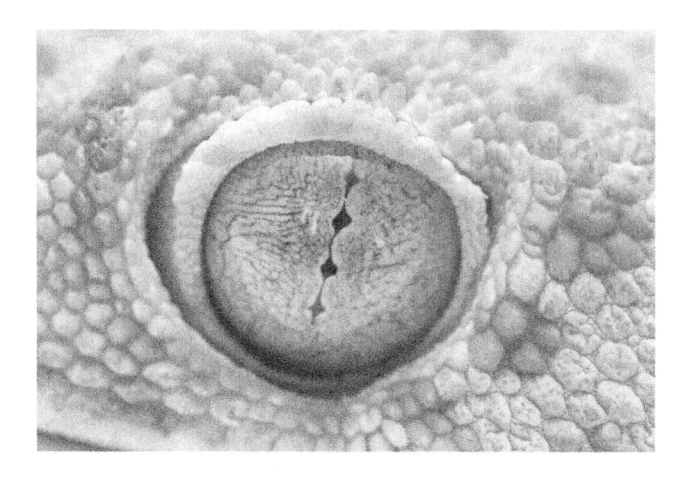

Geckos have unique, vertical, beaded pupils that help them hunt even at night. Animals with vertical, beaded pupils include geckos and certain fish. In strong light, these pupils can contract to very small, vertical slits, with many pinholes emerging.

Each of the beads works together to help the animal assess distance and hunt in a variety of situations. This pupil shape is more common in animals that are nocturnal or active both night and day, and that do not stand too high off the ground.

Geckos are amazing acrobats and they can even walk upside down on ceilings without the need of glue or suction cups. The secret to gecko foot adhesion is a technique known as contact splitting.

Gecko toes are coated with plates called lamellae and are covered with millions of ultrafine hairs and hair tips called setae, which briefly rearrange electrons on the surface they are walking on, resulting in an electrodynamic attraction.

Geckos' feet have around 500,000 of these setae, each of which is divided into 100 to 1,000 spatula-shaped mini-bristles.

The common basilisk lizard has the remarkable ability of being able to run on water, thus gearningthe nickname the Jesus lizard. Because of its high speed and small weight, it can attain speeds of up to 15 mph.

The Jesus lizard has large toes on its rear foot and skin fringes that unroll in the water to generate small air pockets under its feet for lift. This allows the lizard to run through the water and evade predators.

The lizard's fringed feet are one of numerous adaptations that allow it to run on water without sinking. Basilisk lizards use their incredible ability to flee on water when attacked by predators.

Younger lizards can sprint for 10 to 20 metres on water, however, adults can only span a few metres before sinking. They are also excellent swimmers, with the ability to stay underwater for up to 30 minutes.

Did you know that lizards have some pretty incredible techniques up their sleeves for defending themselves from predators? One of the most prevalent methods is to drop its tail, which can distract a predator and allow the lizard to flee.

You might be wondering how lizards get rid of their tails in the first place. It turns out, lizards are born with a weak spot in their tail, known as a fracture plane. When a specific place on the tail is hit or pressed, the muscles along the fracture plane tear apart, causing a reflex muscular spasm.

Because the muscles are pulled apart, the tail comes off along the zone of weakness. But don't worry, no blood will be lost, and the tail will regrow in time, usually between six months and a year.

You would not think that biting your own tail could act as a defence mechanism, but for some species of lizard, it does.

Tail biting has varying benefits depending on the lizard species. Some lizards bite their tails to make themselves appear larger. Others do it when they curl up to protect the soft skin on their bellies.

The armadillo girdled lizard bites its tail to reveal its spiky, razor-sharp armour, deterring predators from attempting to eat it.

Chameleons can use monocular vision, meaning their brains can interpret pictures from both eyes independently.

This is not unique in the animal world, but chameleons are the only animals that can shift their eyes in separate directions while collecting two visual images at the same time.

When a chameleon detects its prey, it can swivel both eyeballs forward for immediate binocular vision too, allowing it to accurately send out its tongue to catch its next meal.

Scientists at Haifa University in Israel revealed that chameleons' eyes operate very effectively together. Each eye serves a purpose, with one eye following the target and the other determining which target to pursue.

Despite the fact that each eye moves independently, the brain understands what both eyes are viewing and collaborates to manage them.

This is being studied to help humans learn how to design robots such as self-driving cars, which require the ability to view several objects at once

Did you know that chameleons have some of the strangest feet on the planet? They are the only animals with entirely horizontal feet, with toes protruding from each side of the sole.

Chameleon feet are zygodactyl, a fancy name for having two toes that stick out to each side of the foot.

Chameleons live in trees and huge shrubs, so they must be able to grip tightly in order to prevent themselves falling. Their horizontal feet allow them to completely wrap their toes around branches and grasp tight.

Chameleons' feet not only assist them to hang onto branches, but they also help defend them from predators.

Birds are chameleon's principal predators, but its grasp makes it difficult for even large birds to pull the chameleon off a branch. So its feet function as a built-in safety device.

The skin of a chameleon is unique in that it is able to change colour to blend in with its surroundings. This is due to specialized cells in the skin called chromatophores which make the skin change colour.

Strange sea creatures

Did you know that dolphins have crescent-shaped pupils that allow them to see very clearly underwater?

Dolphins, stingrays, catfish and flatfish have crescent-shaped pupils that let them view sa very wide area around them.

They can view predators and prey without having to move their heads.

The wonderful thing about crescent-shaped pupils is that they also allow these creatures to see more clearly while submerged in water.

Water may distort and blur things, but the crescent shape helps to decrease that distortion.

This indicates that animals with crescent-shaped pupils have a significant advantage over other marine species.

There are 36 species of dolphins found throughout the world in both the sea and in freshwater.

Many dolphins love to blow bubbles. They use bubbles to herd fish up to the surface of the water. Some dolphins also whack their tails on the surface of the sea to stun fish so that they can catch and eat them more easily.

The narwhal is sometimes called the unicorn of the sea because of its long and majestic single horn. However, this horn is actually an elongated tooth or tusk which can grow as long as nine feet.

Weirdly, this is the only tooth that a narwhal has. There are no visible teeth at all inside the narwhal's mouth. Narwhals do eat large fish but swallow them whole.

The tusk does not appear in all narwhals. In general, only males have them, and not all of them have tusks that develop to such lengths.

A few female narwhals may have shorter tusks as well, although they are not always noticeable. The tusk of a narwhal has a peculiar left-hand spiral that makes it easily identifiable. As the tooth grows, it twists into its distinctive shape.

The elephantnose fish is one of the oddest-looking underwater creatures. It is found in the wild in freshwater throughout West Africa, but now is also a common aquarium fish.

Most of the time, you'll find it swimming near the bottom of the river, probing for food with its long nose which can grow up to 14 inches long.

But here's another interesting fact: the nose is actually a chin! It's not just any chin though, this chin is filled with electroreceptors that aid the fish in navigating.

Elephantnose fish release short electrical pulses from an organ within their tail. Elephantnose fish have poor eyesight, so sensing electrical charges on their chin is essential for navigating the tank or river.

Octopuses have eight appendages, but don't call them tentacles or you might offend the octopus.

These are actually called arms as they have suckers all the way down. Strictly, tenacles have suckers only at the furthest ends.

Octopuses are very intelligent creatures. They can use tools and be trained. They have suckers on their arms that form a seal with whatever they contact, allowing them to grip tightly.

Octopus suckers are being studied by scientists in order to create medicinal adhesives and better robot attachments.

Some octopuses have been observed stacking coconut shells to create a mobile house, while others have been observed opening jars to get to food.

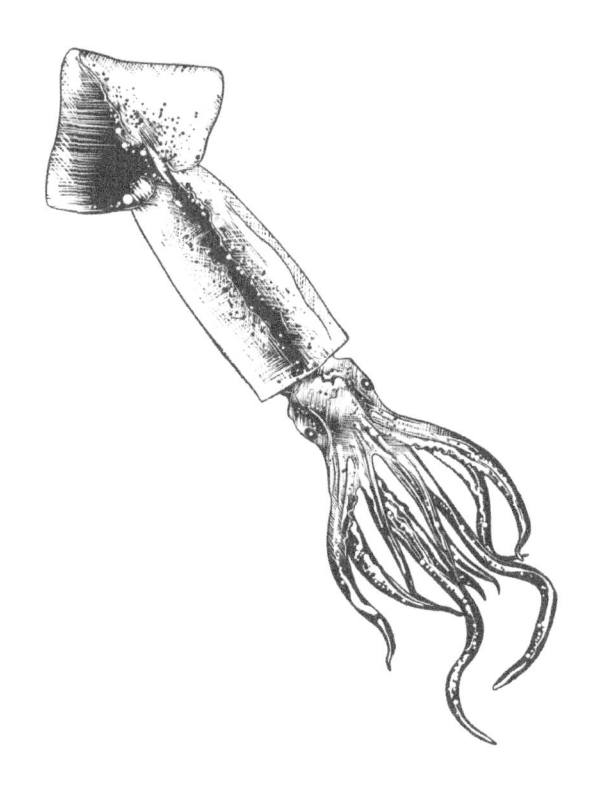

The giant squid is a remarkable creature of the deep ocean. They can be up to 40 feet long and they have two enormous eyes, about 10 inches in diameter, roughly the size of a soccer ball. The giant squid has light organs on each of its eyes, which act as built-in headlights.

The light generated by these organs is a sort of bioluminescence caused by a chemical process involving microorganisms. This type of light is seen in many deep-sea species, and it allows the enormous squid to see its prey in the dark.

But why does the giant squid require such massive eyes? It turns out that giant squid reside in extremely deep ocean waters, around 1,000 metres below the surface of the sea, where sunlight does not reach.

Human eyes have a visual threshold that allows them to perceive light only to a depth of 500-600 metres.

As a result of its large eyes and pupils, the giant squid is able to gather every single photon of light in the extraordinarily deep and dark seas where it dwells.

Scientific research reveals that giant squids' large eyes can identify a moving sperm whale from 394 feet away.

Sea snakes look amazing as they slither through coral or swim in looping shapes through open water. They truly are amazing sea creatures in that they can breath through their skin as well as using their one long lung.

It is thought that most sea snakes absorb about 25% of their oxygen needs directly from oxygen in sea water which is absorbed into their blood via their skin.

One species of sea snake, *Hydrophis cyanocinctus,* also has a hole in its head through which it absorbs oxygen. It is the only sea snake to have this type of gill.

One lung? Yes! Like almost all snakes, sea snakes have one single, very long lung. In most species, one breath through their nose at the surface can last around 30 minutes, however, some species of sea snake can stay underwater for hours.

More marvellous mammals

The largest nose on any primate is the magnificent snout of the proboscis monkey.

Scientists believe that the large nose and nostrils help make the male proboscis monkey's cries louder and more impressive to female monkeys.

Both male and female proboscis monkeys have large noses, but the males' noses are unusually large and can even hang down over their lips.

The males must sometimes get their noses out of the way before they can eat. When they are enthusiastic or angry, their nostrils enlarge and get red.

When they detect danger, proboscis monkeys make extremely loud honking noises, causing their nostrils to shoot out straight.

Even though they may not appear beautiful to humans, their large noses and bellies make males more appealing to female monkeys.

Reindeer eyes change colour according to the seasons. This is just one of the reindeer's clever adaptations to suit its life in snowy northern lands.

In the summer, reindeer eyes are a dazzling yellow-gold colour. But when winter arrives, their eyes turn a gorgeous blue.

This shift in eye colour allows reindeer to see better in the winter when it is constantly dark. The blue tint aids them in seeing the short, blue wavelengths of light that are more prevalent in the Arctic cold. This allows them to find food and avoid predators.

Reindeer's eyes feature a specific component called the tapetum lucidum that allows them to see better at night.

The tapetum lucidum does not exist in humans, although it has been observed in animals such as cats, dogs and raccoons. It reflects light that passes through the eye back toward it, allowing the eye to view it again.

In reindeer, the fibres of the tapetum are loosely packed together during summer, allowing them to reflect light in a wide spectrum of hues.

However, in winter, the tapetum fibres pull in more tightly together and only reflect blue light.

The funny little jumping monkey called the tarsier also has amazing eyes. Each of the tarsier's eyes are the same size as its entire brain.

The tarsier, which is native to Southeast Asia, is famous for its enormous eyes, which are the biggest in relation to body size of any mammal.

Tarsiers cannot move their eyeballs around as humans can because their eyes are so large. Instead, they must move their necks to glance about, as owls do.

Tarsiers can spin their heads 180 degrees in each direction because of this. Tarsiers are carnivorous and hunt at night, so their large eyes are essential for seeing their prey.

The aye-aye is a fascinating creature that lives in Madagascar's rainforests. It is the world's largest nocturnal primate.

The aye-aye's very long and skinny fingers are used to tap on trees to detect grubs under the bark. This is known as percussive foraging.

The aye-aye finds a hollow section of a tree and then nibbles through the bark and uses its middle finger to look for grubs and insects within the cavity.

Wolves howl as if they are singing in choirs, though the sounds they make are not as sweet! Wolves howl to communicate with other members of their group.

According to research done in 2013, wolves tend to howl more to a pack member with whom they have a deep social relationship.

When wolves howl in unison, it sounds like a giant group singalong. Each wolf has its own distinct howl, but when they howl together, the harmony of their separate howls creates the illusion that the pack is much bigger than it is.

Wolves may hear another howl from six to ten miles away in open terrain.

Other types of vocal communication used by wolves include barking, whining and growling. Barking is a warning signal, but whimpering is frequently used to express surrender to a more dominant wolf.

Growling also serves as a warning and might signify dominance or possible aggressiveness.

Did you know that colugos can glide from one tree to another in the forest? And although they are also called flying lemurs, they are not related to lemurs at all.

Colugos glide effectively because they have a thin layer of skin called a patagium that connects their limbs, their bodies, and a portion of their tails. This skin works as a parachute.

Colugos can glide up to 360 ft from a single leap and can travel up to two miles every night. On average, for every metre they descend, they can glide about 40 ft horizontally.

Colugos glide for two reasons. The first is to avoid predators. If they detect danger, they will take to the skies and glide to safety.

The second is to find food. They eat largely nutrient-poor leaves and gliding allows them to move fast from tree to tree to locate more food with minimum effort.

This is a lemur. You can see it looks nothing like the colugo. Lemurs only live in Madagascar. They live in matriarchal groups of around 15 – 25 lemurs.

Monkeys come in all shapes and sizes, and, whilst almost all have tails, there are only two groups whose tails function almost like a fifth limb.

These are called prehensile tails, meaning that they can curl around to grip objects, especially tree branches. Prehensile tails aren't exclusively found in monkeys. Six distinct mammalian families have them, including marsupials and some rodents.

Prehensile tails are especially beneficial for animals which live in tropical rainforest canopies, which have fewer lianas and more delicate tree tops.

The two primate groups that have prehensile tails are capuchin monkeys and atelines, including howler and spider monkeys.

These monkeys are found in Central and South America. There are no primates with tails like this in African or Asian jungles.

Spider monkeys are very adept at moving with their prehensile tails. They can swing through the jungle by utilizing their limbs and tail as propelling levers.

This enables them to travel fast through and across tree tops, even when the distances between branches are wide.

Howler monkeys, on the other hand, are more wary. When going slowly across supports, they prefer to utilize their prehensile tails as a safety harness.

They're not as fast as spider monkeys, but they are still very impressive as they move through the trees they call home.

About the Author

Seana Smith was born and brought up in Scotland and now lives in New South Wales, Australia.

She studied Classics and Old and Medieval English at the University of Oxford and then worked as a researcher and producer at Channel 9 and the BBC.

None of this prepared her for motherhood at all but she did her best with her four children who are now young adults and teenagers.

Seana is the author of the Australian Autism Handbook, Sydney for Under Fives and Beyond the Baby Blues, all published by Ventura Press.

Also in the Series

Wildly Weird But Totally True: Australia

Fun facts, true stories and trivia about the land Down Under

Disclaimer

All information in this book is intended for entertainment purposes only. Facts stated here are not meant to offend individuals, businesses, companies, organizations, and groups. All reasonable efforts have been exerted to ensure that the content of this book at the time of publishing are all true and verified.

Printed in Great Britain
by Amazon

43397460R00056